# The Construction Alphabet Book

## JERRY PALLOTTA          ROB BOLSTER

Charlesbridge

For Cynthia Baker, a cool librarian from Wetmore Elementary—J. P.

To the many individuals who generously gave me access to their job
sites and equipment to help me with my research—R. B.

Text copyright © 2006 by Jerry Pallotta
Illustrations copyright © 2006 by Rob Bolster
All rights reserved, including the right of reproduction
in whole or in part in any form. Charlesbridge and colophon
are registered trademarks of Charlesbridge Publishing, Inc.

Published by Charlesbridge
85 Main Street
Watertown, MA 02472
(617) 926-0329
www.charlesbridge.com

**Library of Congress Cataloging-in-Publication Data**
Pallotta, Jerry.
    The construction alphabet book / Jerry Pallotta ; illustrated by Rob Bolster.
        p. cm.
    ISBN 978-1-57091-437-9 (reinforced for library use)
    ISBN 978-1-57091-438-6 (softcover)
    ISBN 978-1-63289-519-6 (ebook)
    ISBN 978-1-63289-520-2 (ebook pdf)
1. Building—Juvenile literature. 2. Construction equipment—Juvenile literatur
3. Alphabet books—Juvenile literature. I. Bolster, Rob, ill. II. Titl
TH149.P36 2006
624—dc22                                        2005005346

Printed by Sung In Printing in Gunpo-Si, Kyonggi-Do, Korea
(hc) 15 14 13 12
(sc) 20 19 18 17 16 15

# Aa

**A** is for Aerial Lift. Aerial lifts give construction workers a boost when they need to reach a high place. They make it safe to paint a building or fix a loose wire. Aerial lifts sound like this: nun, nun, nun, nun, nun, nun, EEEK!

# B b

**B** is for Backhoe. A backhoe is a piece of construction equipment that has a bucket in the front and a hoe in the back. A backhoe is good for digging trenches or loading other trucks.

**C** is for Cement Mixer. You can also call it a concrete truck. This truck is filled with sand, stone, water, and cement. The round drum rotates and mixes the ingredients into concrete. When it is poured, the concrete hardens like rock.

Cc

# Dd

D is for Dump Truck. Dump trucks carry sand, dirt, rocks, tree stumps, trash, or almost anything. The driver hits a lever, the body of the truck lifts up, and everything slides out. Eeeeee, EEEEEEEEEEEEEEE . . . BOOM!

**E** is for Excavator. An excavator usually moves on its own steel track. Rnn, rnn, rnn, rnn, rnn, eeeee, SCRAPE! The boom and bucket can swing around a full three hundred and sixty degrees. Rnn, rnn, rnn, rnn, rnn, eeeee, SCRAPE!

**Ee**

# Ff

**F** is for Front-end Loader. The driver and the bucket face the same way—front! This machine is used for loading dirt into a dump truck. Don't ever ride in the bucket. It is way too dangerous.

**Gg**

G is for Grader. Graders are mostly used to build roads or to level fields. There is a blade under the body that is set at a certain angle and height. This moves the dirt. Graders can also be used as snow plows.

**H** is for Horizontal Borer. It can drill sideways. Sometimes it is necessary to lay pipe or cable under a busy highway. A horizontal borer can do that without disrupting traffic.

# Hh

I is for Impact Hammer. An impact hammer can smash concrete and rocks. It can be attached to an excavator or a backhoe. It sounds like this: boom, boom, boom, BOOM, boom, BOOM, boom!

Ii

**J** is for Jackhammer. The hand-held jackhammer is small, but the compressor that compresses the air and powers the hammer is huge. If you live near a construction project, this is the loudest thing in the neighborhood. Where are your earplugs? Dat, dat, dat, DAT, dat, DAT, dat!

**Jj**

**K** is for Knuckleboom Loader.
A knuckleboom loader carries
construction supplies to places
that are hard to reach. It has a
special joint that keeps the load
level when passing through a
window or doorway.

**Kk**

# Ll

**L** is for Laser. Laser is an acronym for Light Amplification by Stimulated Emission of Radiation. Lasers project light in a straight line. They guarantee that tunnels, roads, buildings, and bridges are built perfectly straight.

It is hard to imagine how the ancient Egyptians built their fabulous pyramids without lasers to guide them.

**M** is for Mobile Rock Crusher. "Mobile" means that something can move from one place to another. Crunch! Do you need some rocks smashed up? The mobile rock crusher will come to you. Crunch, crunch, crunch, crruunnch, crunch.

**Mm**

**N** is for Night Lights. Sometimes construction companies have to work around the clock. When work needs to be done after sunset, they turn on the night lights.

**Nn**

**O** is for Off-road Dump Truck. This truck is so huge that it is not allowed on regular highways. It is usually used in mining. A lot of coal and iron ore can fit in its gigantic bucket. Watch out! This truck is backing up. Beep, beep, beep, beep!

Oo

**Pp**

**P** is for Paver. An asphalt blacktop road is made of tar and gravel. Tamping asphalt by hand with shovels is too difficult. The paver was invented to lay perfectly smooth asphalt. Sh, sshh, sh, sshh, sh!

# Qq

**Q** is for Quad-axle Lowbed. "Quad" means "four." An axle is the bar between two wheels. A lowbed is a trailer that carries heavy equipment. Some lowbeds only have two axles, while others have three. A quad axle has four.

WIDE LOAD

**Rr**

**R** is for Road Cutter.
Wow! A giant circular saw! A road cutter is so huge and
so strong that it can cut through asphalt and concrete.
Do not use a road cutter to cut your toenails. Eeng,
eeng, eeng, eeng, eeng, eeng, eeng.

**S** is for Scraper. A scraper is used to level a football field, a road, or farmland. It is different from a grader because it carries a belly full of dirt to fill in low spots.

**Ss**

T is for Tower Crane. If you look at the skyline of a major city, you will probably see a tower crane. These huge cranes are assembled on the job and stay in one place. Tower crane operators climb up, up, up to work every morning.

Tt

# Uu

**U** is for Utility Truck.
Telephone service, electricity,
water and sewer, and gas are called utilities.
Wires down! Lights out! Water main break! Gas line leak!
Call the utility company. Workers will show up in a utility truck.

**V** is for Vactor. Vactors are super powerful vacuum cleaners. They suck up rocks, boulders, mud, boards, and other debris. Vactors are ideal for cleaning up after a flood or hurricane. Croosh, croosh, croosh, croosh, croosh—shhhuk!

# Ww

**W** is for Wrecking Ball. Sometimes old buildings and other structures have to be demolished. A wrecking ball is a huge, heavy steel ball that swings from the end of a crane. Smash! Crash! Boom! Crash! Smash! Ka-boom!

**X** is for X-bracing. During repair, some buildings are surrounded with scaffolding.

Scaffolding provides temporary support for workers and supplies. This scaffolding is shaped like an X. The restoration of the Statue of Liberty was one of the largest scaffolding jobs ever done.

**Xx**

# Yy

**Y** is for Yard Crane. It gets its name because you can park it in the construction company's yard. Workers drive it to and from the jobsite. It commutes to work! But it is too big to go get coffee and a doughnut at the drive-thru.

**Z** is for Zipper. This front-end loader is carrying a zipper. A zipper is used to slice asphalt. Zing, zing, zing, zing, zing, zing.

**Zz**

# A a

Writing and researching *The Construction Alphabet Book* was so much fun, let's do it again. **A** is for Asphalt Reclaimer. Years ago, old asphalt was thrown out. Now it is recycled. It is mashed up, re-heated, and laid down again.

**B** is for Bulldozer. Everyone loves to watch a 'dozer! This machine doesn't pick dirt up—it just pushes it around. One bulldozer can do the work of hundreds and hundreds of men and women with shovels.

**Bb**

C is for Compactor. Uh-oh! This is the last page. You will have to finish the rest of the second alphabet by yourself.

Write a zillion books!

**Cc**